Unbelievable
GRIEF

Incredible Grace

Unbelievable
GRIEF

Incredible Grace

A Memoir

Carrie S. Boone

XULON PRESS

Xulon Press
2301 Lucien Way #415
Maitland, FL 32751
407.339.4217
www.xulonpress.com

Unless otherwise indicated, Scripture quotations taken from the
King James Version (KJV) – public domain.

Paperback ISBN-13: 978-1-66285-663-1
Ebook ISBN-13: 978-1-66285-664-8

Dedication

This memoir is dedicated to my dad, friend, and mentor,
the late Calvin D. Tucker Sr.
Sunrise November 29, 1954–Sunset January 5, 2021

Dad, you have taught me so much. Your parenting and guid-
ance have allowed me to grow and be the woman that I am.
You were the calm in the storm; I surely got that from you.
Thanks for the legacy that you have left behind for our family.

To my beautiful mother, I dedicate this book to you as well, as you show me what a dedicated wife looks like.

To my amazing paternal grandmother, the late Mary L. Tucker; you gained your wings a year after your son in the same month: January 22, 2022. Rest in peace and enjoy your heavenly home.

Table of Contents

Introduction

Have you ever felt confused and overwhelmed by your very own emotions? Well I have, and this is my story. Grief, mourning, and loss are areas of life that are experienced by many. My ideals surrounding grief and this process were formed for me early in my life, in childhood. Many times after a loss as a child, I was left confused and overwhelmed by my emotions, which left me with many unanswered questions. My life's journey would lead me into many more run-ins with death, loss, grief, and mourning, even when I wasn't prepared. A terrible disease would take a dear loved one away from me and change the trajectory of my grief process like never before.

Even though I had experienced various losses of loved ones, I never got accustomed to the pain. I dreaded attending funerals and memorial services, as death is so final. There are no do-overs. With a desire to help others, I would go into a helping field where my experience with grief and loss would be highly nurtured and utilized. The initial knowledge that I gained about grief and its nuances was from real-life experiences. Although difficult at times, I learned how to cope in my own way. Over time I recognized and appreciated the sufficient power of God's grace in very painful situations of loss. One particular situation of loss in my life—the loss of my dad—would challenge my faith and experience with grief in a very difficult way. However, God would showcase his grace in a way that I had never experienced before.

This book is for *everyone*! Grief does not discriminate on the basis of your skin color, where you live, whom you know, the amount of money you have, the car you drive, the house you live in, or what letters you have behind your name. This list goes on. If you have ever lost someone, this book is for you. If you are the one that everyone comes to for help during difficult times, this book is for you. If you haven't experienced a loss yet, this book is for you. If you are currently grieving or mourning a loss, this book is for you. If you just want to be encouraged and inspired, then this book is for you.

My prayer is that this book will allow you the space to use my personal grief experiences to reflect on your own. Maybe you aren't sure what grief can actually entail, or maybe you didn't know that there is support for you during your difficult time. Whatever the reason is, my hope is that you are blessed and encouraged as you flip through the pages of my grief journey. I also hope that my journey helps you understand the grief process better and how to allow God to help you heal while you are in it.

At the end of my book, you will find resources that may be helpful during your journey. Also feel free to utilize the reflection pages in the back of this book to write down any thoughts that you may have about your own grief journey.

May God's grace be rendered to you and yours,

Carrie B.

Acknowledgments

First I give honor to God, who is the author of my faith and the finisher of my existence. I am nothing without you. To my amazing husband, KB, you raise me up, encourage me, challenge me, and motivate me. Thanks for being an amazing covering over me and my endeavors. You are strength to me. To my gifts from God, my incredible daughters, you have been my support and cheerleaders throughout this entire process. You always smile and listen intently to the various ideas and dreams that I have. You give me joy and encouragement! I am so blessed to have you as my children. You all have helped me so much with this vision. It means so much to me. Thanks for praying and loving me through this very therapeutic process.

To my amazing mom, thanks for the love, support, and push you gave me to finish this race. Thanks for allowing me to walk down memory lane with you while compiling information for this memoir. You are the matriarch, and I love you for everything. To my absolutely wonderful siblings, Calvin and NeNe, you always have my back through everything I attempt. Through this process we have shared so much reflection and laughter, and I appreciate your love. To my friend, Karla, thank you so much for being there during this process and being one of the first few people to read the words of these pages. You are such a blessing. To the fabulous teams at Elite Authors and Xulon Press, you all held my hand through this amazing process, and I thank you immensely.

Origins

I was indirectly introduced to the grief and mourning process before I came into this world. I am the eldest daughter of my parents. My mother was carrying me at five months gestation when her mom, my maternal grandmother (Carrie), died due to medical complications. My mom explained this loss to me as a very difficult time in her life while being pregnant. It was the fall of 1980, and my mother was pregnant with her first child. Unbeknownst to her she would give birth to a little baby girl.

My mother shared that she was at work one sunny morning. She reflected back and stated that she remembered there being a bit of crispness in the air. While at work my mom received a phone call from her sister. This phone call was not one that she had been expecting to receive. It was a call letting her know that their mother had a medical emergency and had been rushed to the hospital. My mother left work expeditiously, walking to get to the hospital. Unfortunately when she arrived at the hospital, she was too late. The doctors met her in the hallway outside of the room that her mom was in and gave her the sad report that her mom, my grandmother, had passed.

My mom remembers how she collapsed to the hospital floor and wailed from the pain of getting there too late. My mother explained to me how unbearable this pain was for her. She shared that for the first few days after, she would go to her home and feel numb. She would think about the very last conversation that she had with her mother. My mother says that she had already picked out names for her baby whether it was a boy or girl, as she and my dad had not done a sonogram just yet to reveal my gender. My mom shared that one of the nuns at the hospital suggested that she name her baby after her mom if she gave birth to a baby girl. Well, she did give birth to a baby girl, and I was born. The nun's suggestion had provided a calming confirmation to my mother. When she found out my gender, she decided to name me after her beloved mother, my grandmother.

This particular situation of loss is proof that grief does not discriminate or wait for major life events, such as childbirth, to take place. My mom was twenty-seven years old when she was pregnant with me and had to travel down the road of grief at a time when she was supposed to be celebrating the birth of her very first child. Her first childbearing experience would be impacted in a major way. When my mother was carrying me, she was advised by her physician to reduce her stress as much as possible for the health of the baby. She explained that this was a very difficult time for her, but she continued to press forward. But how many of you know that God has a plan for all of our lives? As a result of losing her mom while carrying me, I was given my grandmother's name: Carrie. During my life I would be told many stories by family members about how much I reminded them of Carrie. Stories would be shared with me about how my late grandmother and I resembled one another in appearance and singing abilities. My mother would say to me, "Your grandmother could sing like a bird," a gift I would discover that I had later in life. How special it is to me that I carry her beautiful name and her gift of singing, although I did not have the pleasure of meeting her.

Grief in Childhood

When I was growing up, my parents exposed me to the death and grief process at an early age. Unbeknownst to them, they were preparing me to live through the loss of my dad many years later. Although I did not understand the finality of death and dying, I remember going to many funerals of family members and friends of family as early as the age of eight. After one funeral I remembered one time I rode in a funeral car, and the smell of it remained in my nostrils for years after the celebration of life. The smell was a mixture of flowers and possibly some raunchy chemical, as this combination made me feel sick in my stomach. As I grew in to a young lady, I would create an excuse not to attend funeral services because of the effect the loss and the nuances of grief and mourning began to have on me over time. Losing loved ones was not something that I had gotten accustomed to. I did think that because I had been exposed to loss so much, I could handle it when I needed to in the future.

Growing up I was taught that death was a part of life, but the grief process itself was not explained to me. I would be told by family members and close friends, "It's going to be all right, baby. This is a part of life; we all got to go sometime." I know that those people meant well, but I didn't want to hear that during my time of bereavement. I would learn more about what the grief process entailed as I got older and attended college later in life. Children are resilient human beings, and I believe that, along with my faith at an early age and family support, this is what helped to push through my complicated emotions during grief. I remember feeling shocked, sad, numb, confused, and nervous after many of the announcements I received about someone close to me passing. As a child I was taught about heaven and told that my loved ones went there after death, and this offered me some hope of someday seeing them again. Of course so many questions arose for me after being told this on various occasions. "Will my loved ones recognize me?" was one of my thoughts.

As I developed in to a young girl, my grief experiences varied. I experienced a different type of grief. One of my favorite male cousins was murdered in cold blood. My cousin, who was tall, always had a beautiful smile on his face. He would always greet me with this smile. He was a fun guy who would throw my petite frame in the air and catch me when he came around to visit. He was a loving son, grandson, brother, father, cousin, and friend. I had gone through the experience of losing family members due to illness or natural causes but never to homicide.

One day I received the news that my cousin had been shot. Not only had he been shot, but he had also died from the injury. All I could think about was, "How could someone do that to him?" My cousin had literally been snatched from me like a piece of candy you're not supposed to be eating during church service. This particular loss, at the time, left me with some unresolved grief. I asked myself if this incident could have been prevented. I remember feeling a grief symptom of numbness. I just sat in my room one day, staring off. I eventually was able to make an emotional connection with the loss and just cried. "What an awful way to die," I began to think.

I had not been able to conceptualize the grace of God at that tender age. I was confused about how he could allow something like this to happen. I did not understand what God's grace was in this situation. Perhaps God allowed my cousin's transition to relieve his pain. Our family did not know what quality of life the gunshot wound may have left behind. Would he have been left in a vegetative state or been paralyzed for the rest of his life? What I realize now is that God's grace had been given. "Blessed are they that mourn: for they shall be comforted" (Matt. 5:4, KJV).

My journey with grief had continued. For some reason I felt like I was beginning to attend more and more funeral services. I would grow up learning more about God's grace in various situations. I learned that when it comes to God's grace, it is sometimes not very clear. But as I grew in my faith, I would learn that God has a plan and purpose for our life and path. I miss my cousin very much. I was taught by my parents that grace is the kindness and unmerited favor of God. I was also taught about God's mercy and that it was when God alleviated someone from suffering.

When I was an adolescent, I had a favorite great-aunt named Elaine. She was so much fun to be around. She was funny and was such a good dancer. Whenever the ice cream truck would come to our block, she would make sure that I got a special treat. My favorite items of choice were the ice cream sandwich and the vanilla ice cream cone with sprinkles on top. I remember her even advocating for me in one situation when I was being disobedient, and she stepped in and helped me avoid getting punished. One day I noticed that my aunt was getting smaller and didn't have that pep in her step anymore. She was also losing her hair. It was the first time I ever heard about cancer.

Weeks and months followed, and she ended up in the hospital, this time for the last time ever. Our family visited her at her bedside. I remember her eyes being closed and all of these cords running from her body to a machine. We decided as a family to stand around her and sing spiritual songs for her. Eventually my cousins and I, who were young at the time, decided that we would go down to the family lounge for some refreshments. We could still hear the melodious and soul-stirring singing down the hallway. But all of a sudden, the singing stopped, and the sound of crying could be overheard instead. My cousins and I ran back to the room to find that my aunt had made her transition.

God's grace had been rendered again. This time he had granted one of my favorite aunts a reprieve from pain and suffering. I was a little older when I witnessed how my aunt lost her battle with cancer. God's grace took away the worry, chemotherapy treatments, radiation treatments, and additional pain. Thank you, God, for your grace and mercy. So you see—I had begun to see the intersection between grief and God's grace throughout my life and thought that I had this process figured out. I did not! "Many are the afflictions of the righteous: but the Lord delivereth him out of them all" (Ps. 34:19, KJV).

Although loss was painful, there was a positive connection that I began to make as a result of attending the funerals: it made our family come together. This was a great feeling. One of the best parts of the family gatherings was the "after-party." This party was called the "repast." The word "repast" means "meal" in Latin. We would get the opportunity to gather at one of my family members' houses to enjoy each other and reminisce. It allowed me the chance to gather with my favorite cousins, and we would cut up (a country term my dad would use to explain that we were misbehaving). We would cut up pretty bad, but we had so much fun. It was our way of coping and getting through a very difficult time.

I come from a family of cooks, and so we had signature dishes that came with each celebration of life. Some foods included crispy, well-seasoned fried chicken, sweet potatoes, yams, green beans, collard greens, potato salad, and macaroni and cheese. No catered foods—all homemade with fresh ingredients. Wait, did I forget the homemade corn bread? Silly me! My aunt Jelisa walked with a cane, but if you gave her a chair, she would sit and cook until her heart was content. This macaroni and cheese with its multiple layers of cheese and buttery homemade taste would make you want to slap somebody after the funeral. Naw! I'm just kidding, but the food was always delicious. And of course the menu varied at times with more delicious homemade dishes. Your mouth is probably watering already, so I won't expound any further.

My Soul Anchored

G rowing up I went to church with my family on Sundays, and my love for the Lord got stronger and stronger as I developed in to a young lady. I was around the age of fourteen when I joined the church. After making this huge step and attending Bible classes, I better understood the decision that I had made. Months later I decided that I wanted to join a church auxiliary. I discussed this idea with my dad, and he suggested that I try the choir, so I joined the youth and young adult choir, and a singer was nurtured. Being in the youth choir was one of the most amazing times of my youth. This journey was very pivotal in my spiritual well-being. Singing was not only my way of honoring God, but it became my outlet, my way of coping and getting through difficult situations. Throughout the years my gift just kept developing and improving. I soon would be asked to sing at different venues and programs. I eventually developed enough tenacity to sing at a home-going service when I was asked to do so. I did it, but it was still difficult for me. I never got used to the death, grief, and mourning process.

As I became an adult, I suffered additional losses, including more family and friends. I felt like I was prepared for the additional grief and loss situations that would come my way. My faith in God helped me to believe that I would one day be reunited in heaven with those loved ones who had died. Throughout my life I learned that there were smells and songs that reminded me of the grief process over and over again. Ironically, growing up I even lived across the street from a cemetery.

When I had my own children, I noticed the reluctance that I had to introduce them to the grief process at such an early age. Although a part of the life cycle, I found myself shielding them from death and grief as much as possible. I remember making sure I had made other arrangements for my children if I was planning to attend any funeral or memorial services. A pivotal death later in my life would change my outlook about shielding my children from a normally occurring part of life.

Interpretation

G rief is the psychological and emotional process that one can experience before, during, and after a loss. Grief does not discriminate, and it does not care what great things you have going on in your life. There is no defined time frame for the grief process. There are different types of grief that a person can experience. I will introduce and discuss some general information about grief, symptoms of grief, and types of grief I went through during a huge loss I experienced in the winter of 2021.

There are physiological manifestations that can happen in the body as a result of grief. One can experience headaches, shortness of breath, nausea, disturbances in the sleep cycle, body aches, fatigue, chest pain, changes in appetite, dry mouth, increased inflammation, and brain fog. When we encounter emotional stress, our bodies activate the sympathetic nervous system. This system helps us prepare for possible stressful or dangerous situations. When a person is grieving, the extra emotional stress on the body can cause an imbalance in stress hormones. A stress hormone secreted by the adrenal gland is called cortisol. A consistent and increased surge of this hormone can lead to heart issues and problems with blood pressure. The human body also has brain chemicals, such as dopamine and serotonin, that help with the regulation of a person's mood. When these chemicals are not balanced as a result of an emotional stressor such as grief, it can impact a person's state of mental well-being.

Although grief is a normal aspect of loss, it can be interruptive and sometimes intrusive. Grief can leave a person with feelings of shock and numbness. Grief can interrupt happy times while you are out with family or friends, having dinner. A flashback or intense memory of a lost loved one can send a person into a crescendo of intense emotions. Grief does not care that you are out running errands. Grief does not care that you may have to get up and go to work or that you may have a family to take care of.

What I have discovered to be true is that the grief process is different for everyone and for every situation. Some may have inhibited grief, where no emotion is visibly shown for the loss of a loved one. On the other hand, someone's grief and mourning may be expressive and uninhibited. In this life, grief can cover a variety of subject areas: loss of a job, loss of an opportunity, and even loss of a marriage. However, my dad's experience of loss included his health, independence, and dignity. Any time we experience a major life change, we can experience grief.

Legacy

Growing up I always had an amazing male figure in my life in the way of my biological father, Calvin (Don) Tucker Sr. My dad was the oldest son of eight children. He grew up on a farm in the small town of Hartwell, Georgia. He worked on the farm and matriculated through the Hartwell school system, and then later he moved to Baltimore for work. Years later he would meet my mom, and they would have three children. My dad was everything that a daughter could dream of. He was smart, intelligent, stern, patient, and a comedian without trying to be funny. He enjoyed sports, powerlifting, watching Western movies, serving the Lord, and being with his family.

My dad was there for *everything*! Birthdays, school functions, bumps and bruises when I fell and suffered broken bones during my tomboy phase (yes, me), graduating from college(s), getting my first car, getting married, baby showers, having children, and starting a business. I could go on and on because he was always there. He was such a great man. My dad introduced me to my Lord and Savior Jesus Christ and the youth and young adult choir at church. My dad enjoyed seeing my siblings and me in the choir, as the Lord had gifted each of his three children with the gift to sing. Wonderfully, I am an alto, my sister a soprano, and my brother a tenor. I later found out, after hearing my dad sing in the kitchen one day, that he was a bass.

My dad enjoyed when I was chosen to lead songs, especially the song by artist Kirk Franklin, "The Storm Is Over Now." I remember how I would sometimes overhear him trying to sing his version of the various songs. His tone was off-key, but that was ok, as this was his personal concert. My dad was a handyman and loved the color blue. I believed that he could fix almost anything. Whenever my bike had a flat, he would fix it. If my television stopped working, he would fix it. My dad also built a picnic table from scratch that still exists today. My dad tried to have many of his possessions colored in his favorite hue of blue. He even had a blue lunch box. He had a blue Chevrolet Caprice that we enjoyed riding in.

My dad had a very weird fashion style that my siblings and I would get a great laugh out of. He loved to wear his belt buckle sideways and was convinced that the world was going to catch on to his fashion fad and start rocking it. His fashion idea never took off, but he was adamant that this was the way to go with the belt. My dad was very prideful about his appearance. He would even iron his jeans sometimes with that profound crease.

He always talked about "brogans." We would be like, "What is that?"

He would explain that, basically, they are a heavy ankle boot that he wore for work. When we would say work boots, he would say, "No, brogans." Even when we questioned his fashion choices, he would make light of the discussion and remain adamant that he was styling and profiling.

During the many times that I had the opportunity to speak with him, there was always a lesson. I definitely learned a lot from my dad. He was so passionate about giving advice, even unsolicited at times. I must admit that the lessons were those that I continue to use even as an adult. My siblings and I respected the knowledge from Dad, but we sometimes laughed sarcastically and would say, "Oh boy, here he goes again." Some of my dad's favorite sayings still ring clear to me today. Please allow me to translate them for you. They make me laugh unconstrainedly, and I even find myself saying some of these to my very own children.

My dad would say these statements to me: "Go to bed at nine, get up on time." Growing up it was a daily struggle for my dad to wake my siblings and me up in the morning for school and church. He would come into our rooms and announce, "Rise and shine, youngins." I remember we would act like we were getting up as long as he was standing there, and then when he left the room, we would run back in our rooms and jump back into the bed to try and get some extra sleep. Some days my dad would try his plan B; he would take a face cloth and douse it with cold water and put the cloth on our faces to try to wake us up. Funny enough, that would work to wake us up. It got to a point where, if we heard the water running, we assumed he was preparing the cold cloth, and we would jump right up and get ready for school. He would always be chanting this statement, encouraging us to go to bed early to prepare for getting up on time the next day.

My dad was a fan of education and hard work. I suppose it was his humble beginnings of working on a farm that contributed to the values and morals of hard work and dedication that he instilled in us. He worked every day to provide for his family. Whenever I would try to complain or make an excuse for not wanting to do what I needed to do, he would say, "Work hard in life, be kind to people, and God will do the rest." My dad was a man of principle and excellence—sometimes to a fault, I thought. I was a good student growing up and brought home good grades.

One day, in high school, I had brought home my report card with a big grin on my face. I was so proud of my efforts. My dad said, "Let me see what ya got." He scoured it with an inquisitive look on his face. Both of his eyebrows crumbled with anticipation. So of course my heart started beating fast because I felt like something was wrong. He took his finger and scrolled down the report card and showed me all of the Cs and Bs and asked, "What happened to the As?"

In the back of my mind, I would be like, "Sir, do you know how hard I had to work for these grades?" Of course I did not say that to my dad. I knew better than to do that, but a girl can think, can't she?

I sometimes wondered how in the world my dad could remain so calm in certain situations. My dad had what the Bible refers to as "the peace that passeth all understanding." He was such a calm and collected man. The world could be in a whirlwind, and he would know a calm way to respond. When I was a child, I remember how I came into the house crying my eyes out one day because I was going down a hill on skates and couldn't stop, so I used the wall as a stopper. It stopped me, all right, when I hit the wall—*bam*! I had used my dominant arm to brace the impact and broken it. Ouch! Of course, I ran into the house crying in pain, and my dad saw how scared I was; he remained so calm. He gathered our belongings, and we went to the emergency room (it was called the ER when I was growing up; now it's ED for emergency department). He would always encourage me, saying, "God won't put more on you than you can bear; put it in his hands."

I would be like, "Wow. He is so calm. I would have passed out if I was a parent at the time and had to deal with a situation like this."

We all have a past, and when I was coming up, there were times when my siblings and I were hardheaded. Yes, I have traveled down the road of rebellion, just as others may have. My dad would say, "Y'all are so cotton-picking hardheaded."

I would think to myself, "What kind of hardheadedness is that?" But when I thought about it, my dad was from the South, and as a young boy, he picked cotton, as he was raised on a farm with his parents and siblings. This sentiment likely represented a difficult moment in history that he experienced as a young boy, which caused him to relate it to his children's disobedience.

My dad taught me the basics of financial literacy, even though I didn't understand most of it. In an attempt to help me be financially responsible, he helped me open my first bank account. My dad instilled in me the skill of saving as a teenager. I was excited to have my very own account, as this meant I was doing big-girl stuff. I was still learning the nuances of withdrawals, deposits, and bank fees. I wasn't quite good at balancing my account and had overdrawn funds one day. As a result I had incurred charges that I didn't agree with. The bank denied my appeal, and the fees stood. Impulsively, I closed down my account, thinking that I was doing something big. (This was against my dad's advice, of course.)

Growing up I leaned on my parents and elders for advice. My dad was very happy to help in this area, as I mentioned before. I remember how I would come to him with one plan about a decision I had made in life. I would have thought about this plan and would have had detailed information about it and, to me, would be ironclad. He would look it over and simply ask, "Where is your plan B?" as he flipped the paper back and forth. I would tell him that I didn't have one. With patience he would respond, "Always have a plan A, B, and C." Today I try to execute this knowledge and most often have backup plans. My dad did have very strong ideas. When I contested them, we would have a discussion. And of course, you know the teenage mind thinks it's always right. I believe that I inherited my strong mind from him. I would continue to disagree with something he said during a disagreement, and he would respond with impatience: "You don't get it, do you?"

The Protector

Growing up my dad was one of my protectors. I always felt safe around him. My dad protected all of my family. We would joke with my dad because his stern manner would cause some to pause and question if he had served in the military; he had not.

My dad always had my back, sometimes in a comical way. When I was a teenager, I had worked and saved up to buy my first car. I definitely took my dad along with me during my car search because he had so much knowledge about cars. So we took various weekends and visited a few used car lots. My dad wanted me to have a car before I started junior college that fall semester. We found a car at a used car lot, and I was so happy. My dad taught me about the simplicities of life, and so a used car was like a brand-new one to me. As time went on, I thought about ways to make improvements to my used car. I worked and saved up again and bought myself a brand-new Sony radio system for my car. I was told by the salesman to be sure to remove the detachable face and store it in its case before the end of each day. I was told that this was done to prevent theft of this much-sought-out piece of equipment.

For a while I had been following the advice and removing the face of the radio each day. However, like some things, I had gotten lazy about this task. So one night I had failed to remove the face of my car radio. And guess what? The next morning I woke up to my car having been broken into. And of course I was upset. My hard work had been taken advantage of. Naturally, we contacted the police. An officer arrived on the scene, then he came in and sat at our kitchen table to gather the details of the incident. During this time my family and I were asking where my dad had gone. My brother looked out of the window and told us that Dad was outside at the car. We all asked aloud, "What is he doing out there?" When my dad came into the kitchen, we asked, "What were you doing outside?"

My dad, with a serious look on his face, told us, "I was outside, checking the car for fingerprints." We were all laughing hysterically.

At that moment the police officer stopped writing his report and looked up at my dad with confusion, his eyebrows raised. My siblings and I spoke among ourselves and then blurted out a nickname in unison. We called him "Danger Dad." We even used our harmonious voices at one point to sing the words as a song. The police officer began laughing uncontrollably; he almost fell out of the chair. He was beside himself. I'm sure he probably thought that if we already had a detective on the scene, he didn't need to show up. We all laughed hysterically. For years my dad never lived this nickname down. If a different situation warranted it, when he was acting like an official member of law enforcement, this nickname would be pulled out for additional laughter. My dad would just shake his head in comical disgust.

My dad joined his church security ministry. It wasn't long before he was promoted to chairman of the security ministry. This particular move took "Danger Dad" to another level. Perhaps he had watched too many Westerns and thought he was an honorary member of law enforcement. And yes, eventually he would earn a new name from us. My dad did everything with pride and dignity. We renamed him "Top Flight." I honestly had no idea how important this new nickname would become and how it would be used in the end. Keep on reading, and you will see why I say this. My dad took his role as security guard very seriously. He even sacrificed being able to sit in on church services most times, as he would be outside, ensuring everyone's safety.

He would greet members and visitors with a smile and wave. He would pause the traffic so that people could safely cross the street to enter the church. I remember one incident when my dad witnessed a hit-and-run in front of the church and pursued the suspects on foot in his church shoes. My dad was so dedicated and faithful to his duties as security that he would not leave church until most people safely got into their vehicles and left for their next destination. You rocked, Chief!

The Gifts

My dad was a great mentor to all who encountered him. Whether it was his nieces and nephews or friends and work colleagues, he was always willing to help anyone. My dad enjoyed his role as a baseball coach for Little League baseball. This sport was something very special to him, as he felt like he was being a positive role model. My dad was also a very physically fit guy. He was a professional powerlifter and arm wrestler. I remember swinging on his biceps as a little girl, and he would carry me up a few steps on his arm. I remember going to his arm-lifting and powerlifting competitions. He had accumulated over a hundred trophies from his victories and was well known in the sport of bodybuilding. He later did coaching and competition consulting with one of his closest friends. My dad was still weight lifting and competing into his sixties. I remember one of his favorite breakfast meals was bran cereal with sliced bananas on top. I could never get down with this meal but respected his healthy eating choices. My dad ate healthy and exercised regularly. He had a youthful look and never looked his stated age. He even built himself a home gym with all the equipment needed, complete with a weight lifting bench that he had hand built.

My dad also loved the Lord, and he was very humble in all that he did. He never wanted to be acknowledged for his gifts. He was only concerned about what God thought about his offerings. Every Sunday he would take my brother and me to church; my sister would come along some years later. At some point, if I wasn't going to church with him, I was going with another family member. He never cared, as long as I was going to church, period. I was introduced to my Lord and Savior Jesus Christ at an early age. This experience definitely shaped who I grew up to be in this world. I remember taking that walk of salvation and getting saved. I remember joining the youth and young adult choir, where my gift of singing would be birthed and nurtured.

My dad walked me down the aisle at my wedding. This is a very special element to a bride on her special day, at least it was for me. I remember how beautiful my wedding day was. It was a partly sunny day with momentary sprinkles of liquid sunshine. My dad was there at every step. The men of the wedding party wore crisp-white tuxedos. My dad naturally enjoyed dressing up in suits, so this request was taken on with joy. My dad was very prideful about his appearance. He would shine his shoes, y'all. Ok, back to my point. My dad was proud of his role as the father of the bride. I remember having most of my bridal party stay over my parents' home the night before the wedding so we could get ready together. We had all gotten dressed and were getting photos taken by the photographer.

My dad had gotten ready and stepped into the living room. We all got a glimpse of this king in our midst, dressed in an all-white tuxedo in our midst. Immediately, my bridal party and I started cheering and applauding his appearance in an explosive manner. He was rocking that tux. And of course he entertained our thunderous applause and did a turn as if he was on a runway in Paris. I was blessed to be walked down the aisle on one of the most special days of my life. I told you my dad was a comedian. He told jokes the entire walk down the aisle. I will never forget our father-daughter dance at my reception. We rocked the dance without any rehearsals. Dancing with my dad was such an amazing feeling. It took me back to my time of being a little girl, when he would dance around the floor with me. I felt like a royal queen. My dad was very light on his feet—such a smooth dancer. And yes, he told more jokes during our dance too.

As an adult, I felt like my life was going well, and I believed that I had everything that I needed. It is truly a blessing to get to go through life and have two of the most beautiful and supportive parents a gal could have. I had that! My dad loved me, my mom and siblings, his mom and siblings, and his extended family. He also loved my husband as his very own son. And don't let me talk about the endearing love that he had for his grand girls when they came about a few years after I got married. He often used nicknames, referring to them as "biscuits."

Throughout my development, I went through middle school, high school, and then college. I once thought that I was going to be a nurse, but God had other plans for me. I graduated cum laude from a local university in 2005 with my bachelor's degree in human services administration, and years later I would graduate from a historic graduate school. With my dad's blessing from the very beginning, I earned a master's degree in social work. Not long after this time, I secured my first job, practiced for a few years at a local hospital, and then pursued my advanced licensure in my field. In my work I help people get through some very difficult situations. I have seen people at the lowest points of their lives and have held the hands of individuals who could not see a way out. I have helped individuals who were very ill and those who were on their last days of being on this earth.

I really love the work that I do, helping individuals sort through some of the most difficult situations in their lives. My work allows me to have so much perspective and respect for those who are going through tough situations. Little did I know that my very skill set and ability to be compassionate during times of grief and loss would be elevated in this next phase of my life.

I will never forget the day that changed my life forever. But before I get to that point, I think this information I learned from Dad is vitally important. At the end of 2018, I remember having a conversation with my dad where he expressed that, at his recent powerlifting contest, he wasn't able to lift as much as he once could. I just figured it was because he was in his sixties and getting older. He shared with me, "Something just isn't right." In the weeks after that, my dad began to have some increased mobility issues. His legs would give out, and he would fall. I remember him telling me that he was seeing a back specialist for his new experience with weakness and falls.

I thought, "Dad, you will be fine, as you are one of the strongest men that I know."

Over the span of weeks, my dad began to look a little different to me, but there was nothing alarming. My dad was losing weight, but I figured that this was because he was getting older and still working out, and he was trying to remain physically fit. Weeks went by, and he began to lose muscle mass, slowly at first. His pants fit a little more loose than usual. He got various tests, and one test in particular he told me about was an EMG, or an electromyography. Now, from working in the hospital system, I had some knowledge that this test was to assess nerve activity. This test is used by neurologists to measure electrical activity in the muscles. Still, I remained naive about what was happening. Then came the MRI, CAT scan, spinal tap, etc. I was now beginning to think that something more serious was happening. I began immediately to pray for my dad's healing. I remember specifically saying, "God, please take care of my dad."

A-Who?

I will never forget the day that my dad told me the news. It was a beautiful, sunny day outside. It was in the month of April 2019. I had received a missed call from my dad. He had left a voicemail asking me to call him back. But this voicemail didn't sound like one I had heard before, as there was a tremble in his voice. I could hear hesitancy: "Call me back; I have something I need to tell you." So of course I immediately picked up my phone and called my dad back. I remember we were talking, and he started the conversation by saying,

Me: "Hey, Dad, it's Donna." (This is what he called me.)

Dad: "Hey, the doctors have come up with a preliminary diagnosis, and it's not good."

Me: "What do you mean it's not good; what are they saying?"

Dad: "They are saying I have ALS."

Me: "A-who? What is that?"

Dad: "A motor neuron disease. Lou Gehrig's disease."

Me: "Huh? Who is that?"

This back-and-forth line of questioning went on for a while, as I was confused and had never heard of this disease. My dad continued to explain the report that had been explained to him. I had no knowledge of what those three letters meant. And I wasn't sure if my dad had gotten a chance to do any research, as he was very good at this. What I did in that moment was offer encouragement to him. I told him, "Dad, don't worry. This may be something that, if caught early, can be managed." I remember telling him that we had his back and would be there for him every step of the way.

Hearing these words from a man who never complained floored me in that moment. Those words about his ALS diagnosis pierced my soul in a way that I will never forget. I automatically began to feel physiological changes in my body. In that moment my heart began to race as if I had just completed the first lap of a marathon. My anxiety began to take over. "Lord, is it my turn to feel unimaginable pain?" I felt butterflies in my stomach and began to ask my dad follow-up questions: "Are you getting a second opinion?" and "Are they sure?" and "How does one get this disease?"

When our call ended, my wheels were spinning. I could not wait to get online to research the three letters that my dad had just spelled out to me. So after that conversation, I began to conduct online research about this diagnosis, and this is some of what I learned. There are different types of ALS. There is the familial type, in which the person's parent may have had the gene, therefore passing it on to their child. The other type is sporadic ALS, which means that this rare disease occurs at random and lacks a genetic etiology.

Genetic testing later would reveal that my dad had the sporadic type, as there were no familial tracings of disease in my dad's parents or family that he was aware of. For some, the disease only affects the upper portion of the body's motor neurons, and for others it affects the entire body's system of motor neurons. Some other symptoms I read with apprehension were persistent malaise; falls; inability to move hands, arms, and legs; slurring and difficulty speaking; trouble with eating, breathing, and swallowing; and eventual paralysis of the body. After reading these awful symptoms, I began to ponder what this was all about and thought, "How can my dad have this?" In the next moment, I began to pray and reflect on God's word: "Trust in the Lord with all thine heart; and lean not unto thine own understanding. In all thy ways acknowledge him, and he shall direct thy paths" (Prov. 3:5-6, KJV).

Per my research, ALS stands for amyotrophic lateral sclerosis and is a progressive neurological disease that causes the brain to no longer communicate with the muscles in the body. This disease affects voluntary muscle movement and control. For example, picking up a pen to write could eventually become difficult. I read that the disease was incurable. I also learned that it could affect speech and the ability to swallow and breathe. I continued to pray and conduct research. My dad had done some research as well, and he shared some of it with me. He further shared how he learned that Lou Gehrig was a well-known and dedicated New York Yankees baseball player who had been diagnosed with this disease in his thirties. I had heard about a fundraiser called the "Ice Bucket Challenge" but didn't look into it any further. It was after my dad's diagnoses and research that I discovered that this challenge is a fundraiser held to try and help with the development of a cure for ALS.

I put on my advocacy hat and located a foundation for the disease called the ALS Foundation for Life (ALS.org) and retrieved information from the Mayo Clinic (Mayoclinic.org). I had also researched supportive services and discovered that there were two ALS clinics in the area. My dad chose the ALS clinic connected to the hospital where he was receiving care. Once he got into the ALS clinic, he was also assigned a social worker. The social worker and I collaborated and made sure that my dad had knowledge about their ALS support group and access to their loan closet for durable medical equipment.

Omega

I t was the summer of 2019, after my dad had received his diagnosis of ALS. He was continuing to undergo additional testing and outpatient physical therapy. We continued to pray and have high hopes that he would get stronger. This year a very special family event was taking place. I come from an amazing legacy of strong family connections. Every two years my dad's side of the family comes from all over the world to one designated location to celebrate our rich family legacy. We always looked forward to attending the McMullen family reunion. When I was a child, I traveled with my family down south to my grandparents' home in preparation for this historic event.

I loved the family reunion cookout, as it was massive and most times held on the family land where we, as kids, had plenty of space and room to play. Activities like the potato sack race, horseshoes, and our well-known tradition, the fun game of tug-of-war (males versus females) were always a hit. In 2019 the McMullen family reunion was hosted in Baltimore, Maryland. This location was perfect this year because my dad did not have to travel a far distance. However, before my dad's illness, he could drive anywhere, as he was used to driving long distances. At this point in his diagnosis, he was still able to safely drive his car.

At this time only my immediate family and his siblings had knowledge of my dad's diagnosis, as he had decided that he wanted to share this update with the rest of his family on his own terms. I respected and supported this decision. Another fun aspect of this massive event is the family banquet. This is held at a hotel where we gather to play games, do a talent show, have giveaways, eat, and dance, and the much-anticipated academic achievement presentation takes place. My dad was the proud chairman for the McMullen scholarship committee. His love for education made him the perfect candidate for this calling. I remember taking him around to pick up the certificates for the presentation. Let me tell you, my dad was so meticulous and took an extended time making sure that each certificate was perfect. One day my sister and I went with him, and by the end of this extended time he spent in the store picking out certificates, we said to him, "Ok, sir, I think it's time to go now."

She and I both shared some unrestrained laughter, and of course he gave us the side eye and responded jokingly, "Y'all better wait."

At each reunion he would get up and do an encouraging speech about the importance of education and getting and maintaining good grades. After his speech he would present academic awards to each person, name by name, from grade school all the way through college. This year I assisted him with handing out the awards and gifts to the recipients. I couldn't help but wonder if this scholarship awards ceremony would be his last one. All of the award ceremonies were special to him, but I am sure this one was very special. This was the first year his granddaughters were receiving accolades for their academic achievements. It was a beautiful day, and I wondered about my dad's thought process and whether he thought it would be his last time giving them their awards. So many lasts to consider: last family reunion meetings, reunion dues and registrations, prep for the awards ceremony, last family picnic, and the last family reunion group photo. I made sure that I put the certificates up for the girls for safekeeping, as I believed they would serve as memorabilia for them. Only God knew.

The same year, my dad became a member of an ALS clinic that included comprehensive services to help with the transition of this awful illness. He participated in physical therapy there at the clinic, but nothing really improved his condition. My dad then had to wear a boot on his foot to manage his foot drop, which was caused by paralysis in the peroneal nerve, as my dad explained to me. My dad was such a determined and strong man that he continued to go into work until he could no longer do so, as he just kept falling at work. I remember that before his condition became debilitating, I took my dad to an ALS support group hosted through the Maryland chapter of the ALS Association.

It was a beautiful Saturday morning. I picked my dad up from his home, and we made our way to our first meeting. We sat in a room with individuals suffering from various types of ALS. Their caregivers and families were also there. The social worker had all attendees go around the room and speak about their experiences with ALS and shared resources. This was such a refreshing experience for me personally because I was able to see that I wasn't the only daughter who was supporting their dad or family member through this awful disease. I believe that this group had been insightful to my dad, and we got to hear from others about their experiences with ALS.

During this time in my dad's illness, he was still able to walk with a cane and a boot, so some of the members seemed puzzled. They weren't sure of my dad's type of ALS. The members of the group expressed curiosity about his type of ALS because he was still pretty much mobile, while others were chairbound or homebound. My dad was able to share his form of ALS with the support group and share how the illness had affected his ability to do his powerlifting.

I thought about how ironic it was that my dad, who was physically fit and a powerlifter, was having issues with walking. My dad, one of the strongest, healthiest, fittest guys that I knew, was being beaten down by this terrible neuromuscular disease, but I continued to pray and ask God to take care of my dad. After the group session, some of the members surrounded him to hear more about his powerlifting career. It was as if he was some type of celebrity or something, and I was standing by as his bodyguard or manager. After the session, my dad even encouraged a young guy in the group and told him that he could call him if he needed any advice during his training. And of course my dad smiled and felt flattered by his fan club.

During group sessions, families were sharing their upcoming travel plans for their loved ones. There were some amazing and fun destinations being mentioned. This gave me an idea, and I discussed going on a family trip with my dad. My dad remained very simple and headstrong as he usually was, even in his older age. He did not want to go anywhere. I said, "Dad, how about we take a family trip for a few days. I will take you anywhere you want to go."

He looked over at me and replied, "Nope. I am fine; I don't need to go on no trip." My little vision of going on an exciting excursion with him was crushed in that very moment, like a lilac flower trampled on the ground. He then said, "And if you would stop going to Aruba every year then maybe you could save some money too."

I replied, "Dad, I don't go to Aruba every year." The ironic and funny thing was that I had only been to Aruba once. Every time I would share that I was traveling, he would say, "Where? To Aruba?" I am convinced that Aruba is a place he really wanted to visit deep down in his soul, but he refused to confess it.

We left the support group, and I took us to get some food to eat. He later stated how much he had enjoyed going to the support group and asked if I would take him to the next one. Of course I said, "Yes!" Unfortunately, the next group was some time away, and due to my dad's illness progressing, that was the first and last group he was physically able to get to in person. I am very glad that we had the opportunity to attend the support group in person that one time. My dad enjoyed the camaraderie of his ALS support group and his group leader, who was a social worker too. He would later have to join his support group via teleconferencing, as he could not get around independently.

During my advanced care planning attempts with the goal of helping my dad sort through his life, I was met with resistance. There were times when I wrestled with the crossroads between my dad's denial, faith, and hope. "Now faith is the substance of things hoped for, the evidence of things not seen" (Heb. 11:1,

KJV). Prior to my dad's illness, he was a hardworking, dedicated man who had worked all of his life, which granted him an upcoming retirement. My dad was a very strong-willed individual. Please allow me to explain further.

Prior to retiring, my dad had purchased himself a new car in the particular shade of blue that he wanted. I remember how excited my dad was about his new toy. With the progression of my dad's illness came an increased number of falls, which sometimes warranted the help of neighbors, who would come and assist him with getting up out of the street if he had fallen while trying to get out of his car. It had gotten to the point where the falls and tripping continued to increase, and it was no longer safe for Dad to drive his car.

Eventually my dad's medical team advised against him driving, as it was no longer a safe task for him. I can only imagine how difficult it was for him to hear this update. Eventually my dad relented and stopped driving, and we became his chauffeurs. I worked with my dad and discussed his plans for the car. My dad turned to me and said, "I am keeping my car because I am going to be driving it again; all I have to do is get stronger."

In my thoughts I was like, "Dad, the doctors have explained that you won't likely drive again due to the progressive nature of your ALS." I wrestled with this back-and-forth decision-making week after week as I continued to be a front-row seat witness to the disease's progressive manner. I would feel perplexed after these conversations with my dad.

With more time and reflection, it occurred to me that keeping his car was my dad's only hope. This very act gave him a goal to work toward. Getting strong enough to drive his car again was his hope. And even though I had gone by what my dad's medical team had advised, it was not my role to convince my dad to give up on hope. Eventually I stopped shattering his hope and began to encourage him to get stronger. I wasn't intentionally trying to discourage him and was simply looking at the facts. Deep down inside I felt like I wasn't doing him any favors, but maybe I was. At that time that is what I was unintentionally doing by asking him to get rid of his car. My role was to support his hope, and that is what I did moving forward.

2020

My dad's illness continued to progress, but this had not dampened his spirit yet. He continued to be a comedian in his own right. Early in the year, I was having a small dinner for my birthday at our home, and he pressed his way to get there. He rode in the car with my sister, NeNe. When they got to our home, I was called upon to help my dad get out of the car. As my sister and I attempted to get him out of the car, he fell to the curb. He tried to use his cane to pull himself up off the ground but could not. He came up with a plan B: he would crawl to the front door. And to be honest, my sister and I did not have any alternative plans, so we just went with it.

My dad began his journey, crawling his way to my front door. Of course, there was no male person in close proximity to help us at the time, as my husband and brother were en route. As my dad crawled on the cold ground, the comedian turned to me and said, "Don't worry about the fall; go and get me a sheet."

So I asked in a puzzled manner, "A sheet? What do you need a sheet for?"

He said, "I am going to crawl using the sheet. I can't get these pants dirty because I am trying to wear these pants again tomorrow to my doctor's appointment." I stood there in shock and looked at my sister's face. We laughed hysterically. Months later, the holidays would come with their own set of surprises.

The holidays were very special times for my dad. The month of November in 2020 would symbolize for me a very special Thanksgiving as well. Please allow me to elaborate. My dad was using a wheelchair during this time frame. He was not shy about his food intake on special holidays, and being unable to move well did not change this fact for him. My mom, who is an incredible cook, made the most delicious foods for this annual feast, as usual. It was an honor to be able to share this special holiday meal with my dad for what I felt in my heart was going to be the last time. I don't know why I had this feeling of uneasiness, but I did. I tried my hardest to hint around to my mom and siblings my thoughts and feelings about this. We did as we always did: gathered at my parents' home and shared laughter and good times among one another until it was time to eat.

I remember the time we had gathered around to say the blessing over the food. This was the first time I ever saw that my dad needed to sit down in a wheelchair while he led the family in the blessing of the food. He was usually standing and saying the grace with a strong, clear voice. My dad's signature line was "Lord, let this meal be for the nourishment of our bodies." This time was very different but dear to me because, remember, I felt in my heart that this was going to be our final Thanksgiving together. This moment spoke loudly to the physical decline my dad suffered. With perseverance, he spoke in a small, withering whisper—the disease had withered away the muscles of his vocal cords until they were as brittle as an unwatered rose. We listened with anticipation for both what he had to say and the moment when we could all eat.

When the tears welled up and began flowing down his face, I could feel this sense of immense gratefulness as he said, "Thank you, God, for allowing us to gather here for this special holiday, just one more time." My dad led the most beautiful blessing of the food I had heard in a long time. When I think about it, this moment may have been the very first time that I had ever witnessed my dad cry, as he always presented a strong front for me. I quenched my tears on that day in an effort to show strength to my dad. I did not have definitive information that this would be my dad's last, but it sure felt like it. And I had the same strong feeling of uncertainty for the Christmas holiday. When we exchanged gifts, my eyes welled up with tears because I could not help but think that this was going to be the last exchange.

The weeks went on, and my dad's condition got worse. He kept falling, and he needed full assistance getting up from the chair, to and from the bed, to the bathroom, and so on. I remember how I would wheel him from his room to the kitchen for a meal. Sometimes I would jokingly act like I was racing him in his wheelchair like a race car driver, and he would just laugh and shake his head. Because of all of my dad's physical limitations, my mom became my dad's twenty-four-hour caregiver. As we assessed the situation along the way, we noticed that Dad became totally dependent on care, and we needed extra services. We as a family decided that we would enlist additional help, so I researched support, and we had to enlist a home health aide. Additionally, to help with the flow of my dad's care, we received a lift chair, hospital bed, and other durable medical equipment.

During this quick decline in his mobility, he continued to remain mentally strong and would try and do leg exercises until he couldn't do them anymore. My brother would come over to their home and help our dad with his workouts during the week. We kept praying for a miracle. I remember my father saying to me throughout this process, "God is in control." He never stopped joking along the way, but I could eventually begin to see the concern in his eyes. The glimmer of hope that I once saw was beginning to get dim. He eventually needed total care, as ALS had consumed much of his muscle movement and control.

Final Destination and COVID-19

Our world as we knew it was about to be changed in a major way. In December of 2019, the World Health Organization had shared its suspicions about a respiratory disease that was making people ill in China. In the coming weeks to months, the world was hit by SARS-CoV-2, known as the coronavirus. In January of 2020, the United States acknowledged its first cases of the COVID-19 virus, and it was killing people and causing many others to be hospitalized. By the end of January 2020, the World Health Organization declared a global health emergency and a public health emergency and warned the public about a pandemic. Unfortunately this disease made thousands of people sick and caused thousands of deaths too. It spread from person to person via respiratory droplets. The virus caused side effects including but not limited to respiratory failure; lung, kidney, and heart damage; and nervous system problems.

In March of 2020, the world was declared to be overtaken by this awful disease: COVID-19, coronavirus, or COVID. Whatever name one chose, it was still uttered with hesitance, as it changed our entire world and did not discriminate based off of any socioeconomic factors: race, age, ethnicity, class, income, etc. By the end of March, the governor for Maryland led an effort to keep citizens safe by preventing further spread of the virus and ordered a statewide shutdown and "stay-at-home" order. This meant that nonessential business operations and travel were prohibited during this time. The hospitals, of course, were still running. The governor also advised individuals to wear masks or face coverings, to wash and sanitize hands frequently, and to incorporate physical distancing of at least six feet away from another person.

Before my dad's death, he watched the news just like many of us and experienced the pandemic anxiety. I had conversations with my dad about this pandemic, as many of us were processing our thoughts about it. He expressed his concerns but, as a man of faith, held on to the tenet of God being in control. This easily spread virus affected how we had to safeguard ourselves when we were around my dad. We decided that we would do all that we could to prevent bringing this awful disease to my dad. After all, with his condition, he would not have a fighting chance if he contracted COVID-19. We of course would maintain as much social distance as possible, wear facial masks, and make sure to wash our hands during the visits.

The COVID-19 virus presented many challenges as certain areas of the state were on lockdown to try and mitigate the spread of the disease. My employer gave me a note calling me an essential worker to show officers if they stopped me during my travel to and from work during the lockdown. Other major shutdowns were happening: the schools were switching to virtual learning for weeks, there were certain Maryland Transit Administration bus routes suspended, and the public libraries had closed down. Then there was a pivot to curbside services and delivery services for businesses trying to stay afloat.

My dad was to the point in his disease in 2020 that he could no longer get up without assistance. He needed DME (durable medical equipment) and all hands on deck. One of my family members had to accompany him to medical appointments. And sometimes we were asked to wait in the car, as they were not allowing people in the offices during the height of the pandemic. We had to enlist the help of a home care agency, and even that was anxiety provoking because anyone could have this disease without knowing it. My dad was very nervous about having someone come into the house to help him, even if they were wearing personal protective equipment (PPE). Honestly, we all had some level of hesitancy, but it was a chance we had to take, as the extra help was definitely a necessity. We were getting these services in an effort to prevent caregiver fatigue or burnout, which means physical and or mental exhaustion due to prolonged caregiver duties.

The level of anxiety for my dad and family increased as COVID-19 haunted families all over the world. We prayed that none of the workers would bring the virus around my parents, as they worked very closely with my dad when providing home care services. The stories in the media did not help convince my dad otherwise, but finally he relented. During my research I had learned that the disease could cause harm to a person's respiratory system. My dad was already immunocompromised and suffering from shortness of breath, even gasping for air at times. I thought to myself that this was such a terrible time to be going through: a pandemic *and* a terminal illness. During this time my dad had to use a special type of medical equipment. His most recent lung testing had revealed that he had a decreased lung capacity, which caused him to have difficulty breathing. His doctor ordered a bi-level positive airway pressure machine (BiPap), which is a type of ventilator that provides continuous air to assist with breathing. My dad was understandably nervous, as we all were about the helpers who came as a result of the annoying virus. As I watched all of these changes take place for my dad's care, grief remained intrusive, but a different form of grief would present itself.

This Type

G rief came for me in a way that I did not expect. First of all it came much earlier than I was accustomed to. Wait, isn't it supposed to come after the loss occurs? Prior to my dad's transition, I would be personally introduced to another type of grief: anticipatory grief. What's that? I am glad you asked. Anticipatory grief is what one can experience months, days, and weeks before a loss or the death of a loved one occurs. It is most commonly experienced soon after the diagnosis of a terminal illness. Initially I believed that my dad's illness caused me to feel differently in a few ways. I experienced the same symptoms as normal grief, and I was left feeling ambivalent about the ALS diagnosis. At first I felt like maybe there had been a misdiagnosis. I had remembered how convinced my dad was that his falls were due to some form of back issue. "It's probably my back causing my falls; I just need to do some strengthening exercises." I wanted to fully support my dad, so I initially helped him to pursue this journey.

My dad had even given me permission to allow one of my friends, who was a medical provider in a spine center, to review his scans. My friend was able to provide input that excluded any issues with his back. My dad then pursued a second opinion for his ALS diagnosis, which further ruled out any back or spine issues and confirmed the diagnosis. The results of this further investigation knocked our little theory of possible orthopedic back problems right out of the window. Initially I had prayed that it was back issues because there are treatments for that type of medical diagnosis.

Anticipatory grief does not decrease the level of grief one can have after the death or loss occurs. I didn't begin to consciously feel the grief until my dad officially lost his ability to walk and/or stand on his own. I experienced many of the symptoms of anticipatory grief, such as sadness and the despair of losing my dad. I felt helpless at times. My anticipatory grief grew more and more as I kept reading about what ALS could entail. I truly believe that even though I was consciously trying to hold on to hope, subconsciously I began to worry. I thought to myself, "What will it really mean if my dad really has ALS?" I soon had to understand that this disease was taking my dad away from my mom, my siblings, my children, my dad's siblings, and me—away from this world.

At times the emotional despair felt crushing. Sometimes my thoughts were in alignment with my faith, when they were filled with hope and looking forward to a treatment. On the other hand, my thoughts were not in alignment with my faith, especially after we were told by the doctors that there was no cure. I remember reading this fact in the literature, but I guess hearing this come from the doctors made it feel more definitive. My dad's medical team had worked with him and prescribed a medication that would try and help to minimize his symptoms and offer him only up to three months more of life. I kept thinking that this illness was not offering my dad any form of quality of life; even if it meant that the medicine would allow him to live a little while longer, it would not stop the illness from progressing. If he continued, he would eventually need a feeding tube for nutrition, as he was losing his ability to swallow solid foods and drink liquids. He would need an eye gaze machine to help him communicate, as he would be unable to speak or move his limbs to express his needs.

Before long I wondered, "What will my life be like without my dad, and why do I have to even consider this? Could it be my turn to experience the loss of a parent?" I quickly tried to tell myself, "Girl, pull it together. Things are going to be fine." So that's what I did. Each week had an impact on my dad's frail frame, but I remained hopeful.

The weeks went along, but my anticipatory grief did not stop. Each time I visited with my dad, I noticed another change in the direction of physical decline. So much so that I would feel my stomach turn worse than the feeling of being extremely hungry. The one thing about this type of grief is that this was not a precursor for a lessened experience after my dad left but a way for me to prepare my mind to appreciate every moment I had left to spend time with him. On the other hand, I tried to stay strong and move forward; a new update about my dad's condition would chip away at my hope each time. Although I would feel this disturbing chipping away at my heart, I felt God's presence too, for he was there with us the entire time.

I used this stage of grief as I learned to appreciate that this was a part of the "warning" that I believe that God was so kind to render. I once thought about the ways in which others lost a loved one and how they may not have gotten a warning, whether it was through their lives being taken, a diagnosis, or another way. I finally came to the realization that God had been graceful by giving us a warning. The warning was the diagnosis. This diagnosis was fatal, even though doctors had mentioned a life span of three to five years after diagnosis. My dad's physique had diminished way too fast.

One apparent symptom of my dad's disease progression was his quick loss of muscle mass. Before my dad's illness, he was admired for his muscular and toned body. I remember physically helping my dad transfer from his hospital bed to his lift chair. It only took a few weeks of him getting weaker, and then I could not assist any longer with this, as he could not control most of his limbs. ALS is again a motor neuron disease, so it attacks the nerves that allow a person to perform the most basic of tasks that most take for granted, like opening a jar (something I used to ask my strong dad to do for me) and lifting your arms to feed yourself.

When I reflect on this time of uncertainty, I realize I started grieving from the day that I began online research about what the diagnosis of ALS entailed. As you learned from the beginning of my story, grief does not wait. It has no time constraints and no deadlines to meet. You will need to give yourself the space to let it flow. The method you use to let it flow is totally up to you. Don't hold back.

When an unexpected illness like this occurs, it catches you off guard and can put you in a tailspin of worry and anxiety. I remember thinking to myself that I needed to explain to my daughters the reason for the change in their grandfather's physical appearance, which was becoming very apparent. My dad's physique had gotten very small, and even his bones were protruding from under his skin. I found a great kid's comic book from the ALS Foundation that explained the disease and sat down with my children and provided education to them. They were so sweet and kept saying they were going to pray for a miracle. They loved their grandfather very much, so this loss would greatly affect them too. In this moment, I had begun my work of not continuing to shield them from grief and loss. They did not totally understand what was going on with their granddad, but I at least gave them the space to process and ask questions if they had any curiosity.

The drastic physical changes that I witnessed caused me to anticipate my dad's transition. I did not want to have these thoughts, but reality kept trespassing on my emotional space, like a bear clawing at his next meal. I certainly wasn't anticipating his death on purpose, but I believe this occurred subconsciously because it was inevitable. God had provided for me a little more grace. At least I received a warning of my dad's impending transition. The thought of the unknown sent me into a frenzy that made me do whatever I needed to do to spend time with my dad, even though I was exhausted some days. I am sure that I could never compare my time to the caregiving my mom provided as his around-the-clock caregiver while still working a full-time job.

During this time of heightened awareness of my dad's condition, I made sure that I got my dad his favorite foods, we listened to his favorite music, he provided some more of the financial advisement he was known for, and we even laughed and made some new memories. My dad loved baked chicken from Kentucky Fried Chicken. He enjoyed all music, and we even discovered a few years before his diagnosis that one of his favorite songs was by singer Keyshia Cole: "Heaven Sent." I did not have a definitive date, but I felt like my dad would be leaving us soon. At the time of my dad's diagnosis, the doctors had shared that people who received the diagnosis of ALS would die within three to five years. This information was certainly anxiety provoking to me, as it seemed like such a short time. I still felt like I was in a form of denial after hearing this information. I remember how difficult it was to do advanced care planning with him. This is where you sit down with your loved one and they make their medical wishes known, and together you make decisions in the event the person is unable to do so for themselves.

In my work, I connect people with information about the advance directive or other care planning tools. The advance directive is a legal form that communicates a person's health care wishes in the event they become incapacitated and unable to do so. Although this process took us hours to complete, I could only imagine what it was like for my dad, having to make choices for himself about whether or not he wanted to be a full code or whether or not he wanted a feeding tube. We did this process about a year before his death. It's a good idea, no matter your age or health status, to complete a form like this or to put your end-of-life wishes in writing. It is a very difficult task to complete, but it prevents your family or loved ones from the horror of having to make difficult medical decisions on your behalf if you cannot. As a family we completed the form. On another day, weeks later, we then delicately began discussing what my dad envisioned his celebration of life to look like. This part was the worst for me. These are very hard discussions to have, but they are vital if you want your loved one's wishes to be honored. During this difficult process, we learned that my dad wanted a local memorial service and wanted his final resting place to be back home in Hartwell, Georgia.

Top Flight

When I further reflected on the losses that my dad experienced before he left his infirmities behind, I realize that he grieved the loss of many other things too: his independence, physical mobility, career, dignity, social life, and so much more. However, my dad never stopped fighting until the day of his departure. The paramedics shared that my dad was so strong and fought hard to stay alive as they transported him to the hospital.

The Friday evening before my dad embarked on his new journey, I visited with him at his home. I remember being so exhausted that day, but I pressed my way through. I left work and went home to pick up my daughters so that I could drop them off to stay the night with their grandparents. I am so glad that I did, for this would be very significant for them. When we arrived at my parents' home, my dad was in his hospital bed, as he was bedbound at this point. I had told a joke about his sideways belt fashion, and we all shared a laugh. He responded, "Can't keep a man down."

That Saturday morning my husband went to Lexington Market to get one of my dad's favorite things for him: freshly roasted peanuts. Let me explain further. Baltimore, Maryland, is known for its world-famous landmark, the Lexington Market, as it is one of the longest operating markets in the world. It has been a part of Maryland's history since the late 1700s. Before my dad's illness, going to Lexington Market was his weekly routine. He would get up on Saturday mornings, get dressed in his jeans and some type of blue shirt, belt buckled on the side and wearing white Reebok shoes, and make his way to get his peanuts. He had one design of Reeboks that he purchased and wore all the time.

It was Monday afternoon on January 4, 2021, and I will never forget that day. I was at work and had been there for a few hours. I received a call that my dad was not doing well, and that the ambulance had arrived at my parents' home to provide medical support. I immediately scurried from work. My heart felt like it had dropped out of my chest. A hot feeling brushed across me, and I could hardly breathe. I kept rushing the elevator and thinking, "God, please don't let my dad leave. Please not yet." The anticipation of the unknown increased for me as I ran through the building, trying to get to my car as quickly as I could. I arrived at my parents' home, but the paramedics had already left with my dad and transported him to the hospital.

During this time I was trying to remain calm, as I wasn't sure of the gravity of the situation just yet. "And plus, it has not been three years since my dad's diagnosis, so he could not possibly be leaving this early," I thought. My family and I were at my parents' home, awaiting the doctor's updates (because, remember, during COVID-19 they weren't letting any visitors into the hospital). We were advised that we would receive regular calls from the unit he was on to provide status updates to us. We received a call from one of the intensive care unit doctors, who shared that my dad was on a breathing machine that was breathing for him, and that they would remove it to see if he could breathe on his own.

What the doctor said next changed the trajectory of my emotions. The intensive care unit physician explained that they were attempting all of the life-saving measures that they could, but that Dad had not made any progress. A few more rounds of status updates came, and then it was decision time. At that very moment, I felt like I was sinking down into some form of quicksand. The doctor then asked us what my dad's wishes were. I remember asking my mom to go and grab the advance directive form that we had completed a year before. The medical team was able to implement my dad's medical wishes. Because of my experience working in a medical setting, I had knowledge of end-of-life exceptions for visitation during extreme situations such as a pandemic.

I spoke to the intensive care attending and let her know that we were on our way to the hospital. We quickly drove to the hospital and had to take turns going up to the intensive care unit, so we did. As I stood there, holding my dad's hand, I sang to him and played his favorite songs on my cell phone. I had never been in the situation of losing a parent before, but I had been a helper, comforting others many times. This feeling was so overwhelmingly different. I cried until my vision became blurry. I felt this crushing pain in my chest. I was not ready for my dad to leave our family. The irony of a powerlifter in his mid-sixties succumbing to a disease that broke down muscles had floored me. This was the pain of the unbelievable; my dad had left. I realized that he had taken his flight even though this machine with tubes was breathing for him. Oh, the crushing pain that I felt.

When we returned to my parents' home after leaving the hospital, the pain was still very strong. I collapsed on the kitchen floor, crying. After a while of giving in to my despair, a realization took place in my mind. God's grace had been rendered. No more pain and suffering. No more tests, needles, poking, and prodding had to take place. My "Top Flight" had been granted a peaceful transition. The word of God assures us that despair does not last always. "For his anger endureth but a moment; in his favour is life: weeping may endure for a night, but joy cometh in the morning" (Ps. 30:5, KJV).

I remember feeling so numb and uncertain of what other emotions would consume me. It was so surreal; a part of me could not believe that it had happened. I asked God to help me through the situation, as the pain seemed unbearable. The next day came. This was a day my family and I had dreaded, when funeral arrangements had to be made. It was like I was in a daze during this process and had to snap out of it and be strong for my family. Many plans were developed, including the wording that would go on his headstone, especially "Top Flight." Fast-forward to a few days later, and my dad had a beautiful memorial service at a local funeral home in Baltimore.

Family and friends from near and far came to pay their love and respects. Even his medical team stopped by to provide support to us. It was somewhat strange because of the pandemic; we had to do a walk-through. The funeral home had strict requirements, and folks were not allowed to congregate but had to leave soon after stopping by. We made the best out of this very awkward time. He looked as if he was sleeping, to me. He was so peaceful and still. His skin was glowing. He looked like he was at peace, with a smile on his face. Seeing my dad like that gave me some comfort in that moment.

My dad's celebration of life consisted of two services, per his request. Two days after the local service, my family and I gathered in a large van and headed on a road trip to his second service in his hometown of Hartwell, Georgia. The trip to

Georgia and service satisfied one of my dad's final wishes: to be buried back home. This trip and second service had been documented in his final wishes during our advanced planning meeting.

On the morning of our road trip, I was slapped with the undeniable reality that this trip was to put Dad in his final physical resting place. They were my last moments to lay my eyes on his physical form. I'd tried very hard to hold back my emotions for the rest of my family. When we arrived at my parents' home that morning, it was still dark outside. We all gathered in the house to help my mom load up her belongings.

Me: "Hey, Mom, do you need help with anything?"

Mom: "Hey, Baby, I think I have everything. This just feels so unreal."

Me: "I totally agree."

My brother had already taken the van to fill it up with gas, and so we were ready to make our descent down south. My husband led us in a beautiful prayer, and off we went. It is important to note that I had not traveled back "home" in many years. The family reunions were where I caught up with my grandmother and other family members when they were located in states close to mine. Traveling during this time was very anxiety-provoking because of the COVID-19 virus and how rampant it was running, with no end in sight. I did a mask and sanitizer check prior to our pulling off. If I can be candid, I was not totally convinced that this road trip was a good idea, but I had to do it; it was my dad's stated wish. I will be honest: this, to me, was a very uneasy ride of contemplating stuff. Now he would be next to his father, my late grandfather, Robert Tucker.

Although I wanted him to be buried here in Maryland, I had no other choice but to honor his wish at that moment. My dad's Georgia service was an outside service, as we thought this to be the best option while the COVID-19 virus was so bad. The service was beautiful; a majestic bird flew above us, and it was a sign for me that my dad was peacefully at rest. I really appreciated the down-home Southern hospitality as my dad's processional was led by a police escort, suitable for a king like him. It was so nice to share memories with my extended family, even family that I had not seen in a few years. Now that my dad's celebrations were concluded, I was moving into the stage of grief where I needed to rest and try to rejuvenate. Losing a loved one can be physically and mentally draining. I now had to figure out how my life would be without my dad. Part of me felt bamboozled.

After the service we drove back to Maryland and used this time to support one another. We were able to have moments of joy, as we reminisced about the happy times with my dad. We shared many stories about how funny my dad was and even the contagious laugh he had. I want to acknowledge that there were people and families who were not able to host memorial services for their deceased loved ones due to COVID-19. There were mass shutdowns across various states to help combat the COVID-19 virus. My heart definitely went out to those individuals in pain. The inability to complete this ritual must have been such an awful experience during their time of bereavement. This left some suffering with a form of ambiguous loss because they were not allowed the closure that some equate to attending a memorial ceremony. During this unsettling time, I became acquainted with gratitude. God, thank you for allowing my dad to fight long enough in his disease process so that we could honor his life and legacy.

Ouch

I have shared that the grief process had not been explained to me thoroughly until my college days. However, I had no idea that my grief process would be a difficult one. Initially, I had questioned God: "Lord, how can this have happened to such an amazing and physically fit guy?" My dad was in shape, ate healthy, and was one of the kindest and most humble men I had known. How could this be? When I lost my dad, I felt so temporarily lost. It was like my brain had allowed me to dissociate in an effort to help me escape the piercing pain that I felt after losing my dad. I remember the days of telling folks that things were going to be ok when they went through the loss of a loved one. I had asked those questions of why and how—hey, I am human. However, during my time reflecting with God, I was reminded that God didn't owe me any explanation, and just as my dad had expressed to me on his dying bed, God does not make *any* mistakes. I was on my way to spiritual renewal. I continued to pray and ask God to help me.

When I began to ponder this journey, it occurred to me that God had answered my prayer to "take care of my dad." He did! He gave him rest and reprieve from further suffering from this awful disease. The word of God speaks about God's grace being enough: "And he said unto me, my grace is sufficient for thee: for my strength is made perfect in weakness. Most gladly therefore will I rather glory in my infirmities, that the power of Christ may rest upon me" (2 Cor. 12:9, KJV).

In the online research that I conducted after the initial news of the diagnosis, I had learned that people with ALS may eventually need full-time care, including but not limited to the need for respirators to assist with breathing, eye gaze devices to communicate for them, feeding tubes for nutrition, and the list goes on. When I think about it, God granted my dad grace and mercy when he took him. During my dad's last days, he told me again, when he could hardly speak as he was losing his ability to talk at all, "God never makes any mistakes; he never does." You see, ALS eventually robs people of the ability to speak, as it attacks the bulbar region of the brain. As he spoke this truth to me again, the tears rolled down my face, as I truly believe that God doesn't make mistakes, but it still hurt. My dad was tired and frail, and he began to suffer before his transition. Not too long before his passing, we were provided with information about a feeding tube and were researching information about the eye gaze machine and power chair from his ALS doctors and social worker. The word of God also provides some comfort during suffering and his grace of relief.

"For our light affliction, which is but for a moment, worketh for us a far more exceeding and eternal weight of glory; while we look not at the things which are seen, but at the things which are not seen: for the things which are seen are temporal; but the things which are not seen are eternal" (2 Cor. 4:17–18, KJV).

As I mentioned before, I experienced different types of grief. The year 2020 presented me with a new type of grief experience that I had never felt before. I went through the journey of anticipatory grief. During that time, I also felt guilty about having to envision life without my dad. I felt guilty about looking at his frail frame and thinking about his death. It was awful. Although my dad's doctors never gave us a definitive time frame for death, I had researched ALS and read that the disease was fatal. Not only would I lose him physically, but I also experienced another type of loss: secondary loss. A secondary loss is a consequence of losing a loved one. It is the loss that occurs as a result of the primary loss. Losing my dad meant to me that I was losing one of my best friends. I also lost part of my support system, one of my mentors, my life coach, and my financial advisor.

Passage

My spirituality is very important to me. That's not the primary point that I am trying to make. I am most interested in explaining how you can be grounded and have a good spiritual life and still question why things happen in life. When my dad was diagnosed with ALS, I first thought, "He is one of the strongest men that I have ever known; he is going to beat whatever this is." After I conducted research about this awful disease, I still thought, "He can beat this." It wasn't long before I saw my dad's very buff biceps disappear. I saw the fight in his eyes diminish. In the beginning of his illness, I witnessed him fall to the ground and trip. I remember having to put him in the car along with my mother as he was on his way to the hospital.

My dad always presented a strong front for me. I would ask him how he was doing, when clearly he wasn't doing well, and he would say, "I'm doing fine." I wondered if my dad had his midnights when he would cry out to God and ask for additional miracles and healing like Jesus did in the Garden of Gethsemane. "And he went forward a little, and fell on the ground, and prayed that, if it were possible, the hour might pass from him. And he said, Abba, Father, all things are possible unto thee; take away this cup from me: nevertheless not what I will, but what thou wilt" (Mark 14: 35–36, KJV).

Grief presents itself in various ways and is shaped by different factors. Grief can be shaped by our cultural norms and our past experiences. The way I grew up helped to shape my grief response and coping mechanisms. Although I had been exposed to grief at an early age, it affected how I would choose to deal with loss later in life. I began to put up a wall to shield myself from the turbulent emotions experienced from losing those closest to me. I recognized as an adult that to some degree, I buried my grief, as sometimes I thought that it was too much to handle.

For one reason or another, I thought that I was being strong for others by not showing emotions at funeral services. I remember holding back the tears sometimes. After all, I had not seen my dad cry at funerals, so why should I? This level of suppression would form my individual grief response and lead me down a road of disturbed emotional reckoning.

Grief can also be shaped by the relationship that one has with the deceased person. Have you ever gone to the funeral of a person you didn't know to support a loved one or friend? You may not have shed a tear or shared any emotion. This could have been because there was not an emotional attachment to the person. There was a lack of familiarity. It does not make one less of a person, but the lack of a bond determines how you will respond in your grief. The losses I described earlier were those of the loved ones closest to me. They all had a theme: I was affected in some way and exhibited some form of grief and mourning, whether it was sadness, crying, or feelings of shock.

A grief response can be overwhelming and also be shaped by the cause of your loved one's death and your spiritual background. You see, I love God with all of my heart and soul, and I still asked how my dad, one of the healthiest-eating people that I knew, could be plagued with such an awful disease. However, I am human. In my moment of despair, I allowed myself to have the emotion, and then I got myself together with prayer because God is in control. He never left me. This situation was a part of God's master plan. (In full transparency, it took me a while to get to this perspective, but I did with his grace and mercy.)

Help for the Helper

My dad passed within the month of my fortieth birthday. Now, some would say that the "normal" grief process was supposed to begin then. My husband had taken me away on a trip for my birthday. On my birthday I was overcome by emotion as I stared out the window, out at the mountains. About a week before my birthday, I remained in a mild form of shock. One day I was sitting on my bed and decided to clear the saved voicemails off of my phone. And lo and behold, I found a special treat: a voicemail from my dad that I had saved.

The sounds echoed off my ears like sweet, calming tones. "Hey, Donna, it's Dad. I'm just calling you to wish you a very happy birthday. Love you. Enjoy, and God bless." My heart skipped a beat, and my face lit up with joy. And of course, I resaved this message. It was such an honor to have that message and to be able to play it, allowing him to still wish me a happy birthday. I remember I cried like a baby, but I so needed the emotional release. Trying to be strong for yourself and others is very tough on your mind, body, and soul. However, the tears in that moment on my special day let me know that my dad was still with me spiritually and that everything was going to be ok. After that, I was able to go and enjoy the festivities that had been planned for me.

I was not sleeping well after my dad passed. I would lie awake at night, just ruminating on the loss of my dad. I wondered whom I would be able to talk to, laugh with about certain things, and get financial advice from now that my dad was gone. I continued to pray because God had still rendered grace and love during this journey. I remember checking on how my siblings were doing and sharing with them that I was not sleeping. My sister bought me some organic lavender oil to help with my insomnia. I remember times when I would be out running errands, and I would be triggered. A trigger is any one thing, event, smell, person, or stimulus that reminds you of your lost loved one. A song that would trigger me would be the one by Sinach, called "Way Maker." If this song came on, I would just burst into tears. Then I would have to gather myself, wipe my face, and head into the grocery store or wherever I was going.

I kind of figured that my grief experience was going to be different because I've always had both of my parents around—but not this different. I had an amazing team that has been there for everything and helping me navigate through life. As I stated earlier, I was not sleeping, and I cried regularly. I kept reassuring myself that this behavior was ok. Again, crying is a coping mechanism that can allow for an emotional release, so I let it flow. As I attempted to reach for my emotional equilibrium, I called on one of my tools from my coping toolbox: journaling.

As a child I loved to write, and who would have known that this skill would allow the task of journaling to be so easy for me? I was at home one day and decided to pull out a notebook that I had never written in before. This is where my grief journaling journey began. I wrote about all of my emotions, including the guilt that I felt. I wrote about the memorial services and noted my symptoms and goals for self-care. I connected with journaling but continued to have a yearning to further process the overwhelming and unbelievable emotions attached to this particular loss. I pondered whether I wanted to speak with a professional about my symptoms. I wanted a neutral, nonjudgmental person to help me. I finally enlisted a therapist for grief counseling.

Initially I kept procrastinating on my decision to seek help. I kept saying, "I'm going to get through this," and thought that I just needed more time. I reflected on how the helper can need help too. I realized that my human nature made me as vulnerable in my time of bereavement as any other person. I kept trying to rationalize my reasons for not seeking help. In this situation I stepped on my pride, and it was a great decision. I was able to see a therapist and get that neutral support that I was looking for. I was not judged but provided with unconditional positive regard. I was free to share all of my feelings and process my grief response. The pain of it, the loss, was one element I really worked on in grief counseling. I also reviewed coping strategies and self-care tips.

There are different levels of grief, and through this process it is important to first accept that the loss has happened. It took me some time to even accept my dad's loss. Even though I figured God had given me a warning by allowing such a disease to consume him, his transition was still shocking. I believe that I was in shock for a while. I knew that he was no longer present; it's just that I had to get my brain in line with this reality. Then I had to become familiar with the finality of the loss. This has been the hardest part for me, as death is so final. There is no turning back, and there are no do-overs.

Allow your emotions to flow freely. Throughout my life I had held in emotions regarding loss, as I had seen it so much. This is not a healthy choice. However, when this loss occurred, I allowed myself to be uninhibited; I did not hold back. I noticed that I started to cry much less as time went along. Lastly, enlist the help of your support system and don't rush your grief response. I was blessed to have the help of my amazing husband, children, mom, siblings, friends, and colleagues. I was not afraid to ask for help or excuse myself if I needed to take a break.

I remember explaining to the therapist how difficult of a decision it was for me to start the process because of my work in the mental health field. I kept telling myself that I already knew the coping strategies and self-care techniques to be used. I had made an important step and was no longer ashamed to seek help. I did it! I made the call! I did a short-term course and began to notice the difference in my emotional well-being. This was the beginning of what I considered picking up the cookie crumbs—the pieces that death had caused for me to live in this life without my dad, my friend, my homey.

Grief Forward

Moving through the grief process can be an unpredictable tidal wave of emotions. One day I would be fine emotionally, and then another day I would need a moment. One day I was at home in my kitchen, and I thought that I was doing well. My youngest daughter came to me and talked about how she missed her granddad and how she wasn't ready for him to go. I grabbed her and wrapped my arms around my baby girl. In that moment I became overwhelmed with a crescendo of uncontrollable emotions, and so we cried together. In that moment it was also important for my child to see me in this vulnerable state. So many times we, as parents and caregivers, try to stay strong for others without realizing the resilience that kids naturally have. Additionally, children learn emotional intelligence and acceptable norms from their parents and environment. I wanted her to know that it is normal to feel pain and cry as a result of it.

Those tears later became a refreshing river of joy for me in the direction of healing. In a few weeks I had returned to work and kept my coping strategies readily available in the event I became triggered. My therapist had me write down my coping strategies for easy retrieval, which I did not have to use. I did much better than I thought that I would do emotionally. I was able to compartmentalize and do what I needed to do.

After my dad passed, I was initially left in a posture of shock. I had seen my dad in the hospital bed on the ventilator and was notified by the medical team of when this intervention would be removed, but I was numb and powerless. As a part of my grief work and in order for me to move on, I had to wholeheartedly accept that the loss had actually occurred. I must admit, this step was much more difficult than I had believed. As a matter of fact, the initial acceptance was unbelievable. I had seen loss before, but this exit was so glaringly different.

This step in the process does not happen instantly for all, so just be encouraged as you go along on your own journey. In parts of my mind, I knew that my dad was not physically available, but I needed the rest of my mind and body to catch up with this reality. I remember, weeks after my dad's transition, I caught myself picking up the phone to send him a text. I caught myself and was like, "Girl, what are you doing?" It was just so common for us to text on a daily basis, so I had not gotten out of that rhythm yet. With prayer, God has helped me along. Journaling my feelings and realities surrounding the loss helped me ground my thoughts.

It's also important to process the pain of the grief. Initially I could not believe how much the loss hurt. I shared earlier that I had learned how to suppress my feelings about grief, growing up. As I became older, I wanted to tap back in to those emotions, and so I did. When my dad transitioned, I allowed myself to cry. I cried whenever I felt the urge. I was uninhibited, free to let the fountain of sadness and brokenness fall down my face. In these moments of emotional catharsis, I felt a sense of freedom. My heavy chest felt lighter; I breathed again. And with each cry and release, my heart was free to beat again and again. It reminded me of God's words of comfort:

> "And ye now therefore have sorrow: but I will see you again, and your heart shall rejoice, and your joy no man taketh from you" (John 16:22, KJV).

Now that my dad was gone, I wanted to be there for my mom more than ever before. After all, she had lost her soul mate, her friend, and her husband. I would make regular home visits to check in on her. I remember the first time I visited my parents' home after the services were over. There was a hesitance inside of me as I walked slowly from my car to the front stairs of their home. My heart rate increased, and my breathing became labored. I had no idea that I would feel this way when I visited home. I saw his room in a different way because he was not there. On my way down the hall, I got to my dad's room, and I peeked in the door like a child peeking around the corner, as if playing a game of hide-and-seek, not going all the way in.

I was suddenly overcome with emotions, and the tears began to flow. My mom came over to console me.

Mom: "You ok, Baby?"

Me: "No, not really. It's just so weird not seeing Dad here."

Mom: "Yeah, I know. It doesn't seem real, does it?"

Me: "No, it doesn't."

We provided comfort to one another in that moment and for several moments thereafter. It took me a few of these instances before I was ready to walk all the way into the room, but eventually I did. I was encouraged by God's word: "Many are the afflictions of the righteous: but the LORD delivereth him out of them all" (Ps. 34:19, KJV). The hospital bed was still in his room, and the lift chair was in the dining room. We eventually made arrangements for the ALS Foundation to come and pick up the equipment that they had so graciously let us borrow. Days along, I would walk into the bedroom and just stand there by his hospital bed, still in some form of shock and disbelief that he was no longer there. I would no longer hear him in his hoarse voice say, "Donna, go and get me some water, would you?" or "Cover up my legs, please." A few more weeks went by after my dad's transition, and by this time our minds had space to make arrangements, and the medical equipment had been picked up. When I went by my dad's room this time, the hospital bed was gone. I remember how I just stood there because now the bed was gone, and this was a clear sign that he was gone. I noticed that I was able to stand inside the room this time. For a moment I smiled as I thought to myself, "You went on home, Dad. No more pain, suffering, or worries." In that moment I felt gratitude.

As time went on, I would be presented with other opportunities to face the intrusiveness of my grief. About half a year later, I went into my dad's shed, which he used as a workout room, to return some items I had borrowed. I had not been in his man cave for a long time. I put the items inside the shed, and I was captivated by the greatness he had left behind. I marveled at the massive amounts of powerlifting and weight lifting memorabilia, articles, and trophies. I got a glimpse at one of his powerlifting champion belts. When I was a little girl, he would come home excited about his win but humble at the same time.

I would say to him, "Congratulations, Dad. You won another trophy?"

He would flex his bicep in a joking manner and reply, "I guess I am a champion."

I was very impressed as his trophy case just kept expanding.

My dad had accomplished much during his tenure as a powerlifter and arm-wrestling competitor. I honestly did not expect to be taken aback simply by visiting a space that was so special to him. (And remember how I had explained how intrusive grief can be; this was a perfect example, but life goes on.) I surely did allow myself those moments of reflection and appreciation for my dad's talents. As time went on, the crying decreased; my soul was able to release the tears of pain, brokenness, and despair. I was doing what I needed to do to head toward my healing.

Anniversaries

As time moved on, I began to get closer to anniversaries and firsts of not having my dad around. I was not sure how I would handle each situation, but I felt somewhat equipped to go on this ride. I received beautiful support and text messages from those who cared about me, encouraging me and telling me it was going to be ok.

Father's Day would be so different for me. June 20, 2021, was the first time I was not able to celebrate with my dad, which is something I really enjoyed doing. I had even hosted a few cookouts to commemorate this special day. I knew that I was going to celebrate the time in some fashion, as I was certainly going to honor the great father that my husband is to our girls. I had to come to terms with myself that I would not be able to celebrate this day with my dad for the rest of my life. The pain of it began to resurface again. About a week before Father's Day, I was invited to a cookout to honor fathers. To be honest I was reluctant at first because I did not have my father to celebrate. It was so close to the time when I had lost him. I wasn't sure how my grief would present itself. I am not a person to ruin great moments for others, so I prayed for God to help me and went anyway.

The cookout was arranged in such a cute way, complete with a buffet and customized Father's Day menus. I had made up my mind to settle in, and if I needed to excuse myself due to being overcome by emotions and being triggered, I would do just that. I remembered in that moment that I was followed by God's grace and mercy, and that thought served as the impetus to help me cope. I enjoyed watching the host talk with her dad about what he had chosen from the menu. After he shared his desired meal selections, I smiled as she prepared his plate.

I was doing fine with coping so far. I took a deep breath and smiled, as this was totally something that I had done for my dad when he was here. I had no idea that such a kind gesture would impact my continued grief journey so much. I was happy to challenge my reluctance to go to a Father's Day celebration without my dad. Victory and peace were my plans for the day. After all, my dad was still there with me in spirit. One of the meals my dad would enjoy for Father's Day was a delicious steak and chicken kabob dinner. I would add his favorite vegetables to the kabob, like squash and broccoli. He often would enjoy this meal with an ice-cold soda. I would ask, "How is your dinner, Dad?"

He would nod his head with approval and say, "Very good, thank you."

For me this was always a great compliment to my ever-developing culinary skills. I had also refocused my thoughts on celebrating my husband, and I pushed through.

The fourth of July was a family holiday that we always celebrated together. My dad was our grill master; he loved cooking on his charcoal grill. My dad was never into fancy things like a gas grill and just preferred the simple things in life. This particular Independence Day in 2021 was different. We made the best out of the day. We gathered as a family, and my husband had the fireworks as he faithfully did, but Dad wasn't there to tell us when to cut it off this time. We all shared stories and laughter about the different things that he would be doing during this holiday. We all got through the day, but it was very tough. That holiday will never be the same without him.

The major holidays, Thanksgiving and Christmas, came around. Thanksgiving was very special for my dad, as it was one of the days that he ignored his healthy diet and went all in on the vast and delicious feast my mom prepared. He was not ashamed to explain why his slice of my mother's homemade sweet potato pie was so big. My siblings and I would joke around, pretending to take a piece of his pie, and get our hands swatted away.

The first anniversary of my dad's birthday came: November 29, 2021. I remember that at the beginning of the year I had written a happy birthday greeting to my dad in my day planner, as I always did. On that day I received so many beautiful messages from my dad's side of the family wishing him a happy birthday. It was such a sweet sentiment. Now my dad would be celebrating his birthdays from the heavens. Christmas was very different that year. That year my husband and I hosted a Christmas breakfast. After dining we did a photo shoot, and it was beautiful. We all wore matching elf hats. There is one element missing when I look back at the beautiful photos: my dad. He isn't in the photos, but he was there in spirit. And besides, I imagined myself trying to convince him to wear the silly elf hat for the photo op and him refusing. But in that moment, I can imagine him saying, "No thanks to the elf hat; I have traded that in for my crown"—God's crown of victory.

As I look around, my world looks different without my dad, but I am adjusting well. I am in a better grief space now. I am integrating the loss of my dad and am moving forward in my life. This grief is real, and it is a part of my story. This is what my dad would want me to do. Whenever I would try to complain around him, he would pause and give me a look and encourage me by saying, "You betta get up like somebody."

In the beginning each day was an unpredictable ebb and flow of sadness, joy, peace, or despair. An emotional roller coaster, if you will. Each day I am becoming stronger. Grief is a journey, and so there is no stopwatch to conclude its session. My physical dad left, but my heavenly father is still here. Adjusting to life without my dad was a world of firsts for me. I wondered, "Who in the world will I call on the phone to ask the same ridiculous questions about finance stuff again." Let me share another real story. About a month or so after Dad's transition, some finance paperwork came that I didn't quite understand. So without a thought, I picked up the phone to call my dad, but this time I did not try to locate his number. See, I am getting better, y'all, because last time I actually made the call. Real stuff. I laughed aloud and said, "Dad, I know that you are looking down on me and shaking your head."

I would laugh at how off tune he would sing the vamp of Kirk Franklin's song, "The Storm Is Over Now." I would overhear him in the kitchen after church sometimes, singing "No More" with all of his heart. He and I would laugh. Guess what? I still get to laugh. But "No More" is his testimony now. No more pain and suffering. How about that! God's grace has been rendered. Grief goes on, and so does life!

The Aftermath

After my dad's memorial services, I made an effort to try and get back to my life with the many hats that I wear, but it took space and time. There were times when I contemplated throwing away the dress that I was wearing on the day that my dad took flight. A part of me was initially angry (a normal grief response). I was angry that my dad had gone so soon. I just remember wanting to get the sight of that dress out of my face. This goal was my way of coping; throwing this dress out was a way for me to avoid the reminder of the pain. To me, it was the garment that I had rolled around on my parents' kitchen floor in on the night of the loss. It was the dress that I stood in at my dad's bedside at the hospital ICU, and on which I had shed massive amounts of tears. It was the dress that I wore when I felt like I had stopped breathing at the sound of the inevitable.

Well, I guess I just ended up hiding it. I was purging a bin of clothes about a year and a half later, and guess what I found? Yes, the dress. I gathered the dress from the bottom of a plastic bin, but this time I picked up the dress and smiled. I said out loud, "I am so glad that I still have this dress." In my moment and journey of healing, this dress has new meaning. It now represents my dad's relief from suffering. Since then I have worn this dress and marvel at its symbolic nature in a positive way. Thank you, God, for peace! This was now my "weeping may endure for a night, but my joy is coming in the morning" dress. And now I have exhaled.

One of the most substantial grief experiences of my life occurred in 2021. More than a year later, I still find myself adapting to a world without my dad (totally normal, by the way; remember grief has no time frame or time limits). I began penning this memoir in the spring of 2022. My purpose was simply to remember my dad and to help others who may have been in or are currently walking in the grief path.

The intersection between grief and God's grace has been made very clear to me. It took me losing my dad to ALS to receive a reeducation in God's grace and mercy. Although I had believed that my early childhood experiences with grief and loss had prepared me, I was not correct. This grief journey illuminated some holes in my toolbox. Coping strategies that I had used before would not work. Suppressed tears did not stand a chance.

I learned more about my resilience and ability to move forward in the world. The world without my friend and his presence and support. Without his voice advising me against making dumb mistakes. I learned that God's grace is more than sufficient. And just like my spiritual track star had done, he finished his race. I now smile and rejoice and am comforted by God's word: "I have fought a good fight, I have finished my course, and I have kept the faith. Henceforth there is laid up for me a crown of righteousness, which the Lord, the righteous judge, shall give me at that day: and not to me only, but unto all them also that love his appearing" (2 Tim. 4:7–8, KJV). Enjoy your crown, sir!

Tribute

Dear Dad,

I just want to say thank you! Thank you for everything! Thank you for your excellent teachings, even though they weren't always solicited. Thanks for never giving up on me. You were such a great friend and life coach.

Thanks for allowing me some room to flex my wings by making mistakes and flying in life. Thanks for teaching me how to drive a car and for helping me through the process of getting my very own. Thank you for teaching me karate and self-defense. Thank you for being the best example for choosing not to fight every battle but choosing battles. Thank you for the best inside jokes ever.

Thank you for your financial teachings and showing me how to be economical. Thanks for showing me that nothing is impossible through God. Thank you for teaching me to love the skin that I am in. You showed me how to properly work out even though I didn't listen to your expert advice. Thank you, until we meet again.

Coping Tips for the Grief and Loss Journey

The below resources are being provided for informational purposes only.

1. Give yourself time to feel the emotions that you are feeling.
2. Give yourself time to accept that a loss has occurred in your life.
3. Don't allow anyone to tell you how long your grief should take.
4. Don't compare your grief process to anyone else's.
5. Don't put your grief in a box; it is now a part of your daily journey.
6. Pull on your support networks for help.
7. Embrace laughter! Seriously, laugh, laugh, and laugh some more.
8. Do activities that provide relaxation (i.e., meditation and yoga).
9. Journal about your thoughts and emotions.

Some journaling prompts to get you started if you don't know what to journal about:

The loss of my loved one makes me feel...

This loss has caused me to appreciate...

Today my loss has caused me to reflect on...

The best memory of my loved one is...

One way I am going to honor my loved one's memory is by...

I really miss when my loved one used to...

This loss has caused me to become more...

Community Resources

The below resources are being provided for informational pur-poses only.

ALS—amyotrophic lateral sclerosis—a progressive motor neuron disease that impacts how the brain communicates with the spinal cord (ALS.org)

The ALS Foundation for Life
www.als.org
The website also allows you to search for ALS clinics and sup-portive services in your area.

The ALS Association's Care Services Department
1-800-782-4747

ALS Online Resource Directory
http://www.alsa.org/als-care/resources/resource-directory.html

ALS Youth Education Book
https://www.als.org/navigating-als/resources/Youth-Education

May is ALS Awareness Month

Muscular Dystrophy Association Resource Center
1-833-ASK-MDA1 (1-833-275-6321)
By Email: ResourceCenter@mdausa.org
This website is for the MDA center. They also provide resource information to individuals with ALS.

You may contact your local department of aging and inquire about home care resources and durable medical equipment (DME) programs for your loved one.

Need-to-Know Questions and Answers

What will happen in therapy and or grief counseling?
A licensed and trained mental health professional will complete a full assessment about your history. They will then collaborate with you, listen to your story of loss, and help you understand the grieving process. Your work may also include learning coping strategies and how to actualize them. The mental health professional also helps with ideas for memorializing your loved one.

How do I find a therapist and or grief counselor?
Call the number on the back of your insurance card to start this process; they can provide a list of in-network behavioral health specialists. Also discuss coverage benefits and possible costs associated with receiving services. Local hospice centers and some churches have bereavement ministries as well. Call to inquire.

Does going to a counselor mean I am "crazy"?

Absolutely not! There continues to be a stigma attached to obtaining mental health and emotional supportive services. Seeking help during your time of emotional need does not mean you are weird or crazy. We are human beings, and just as God has gifted physicians to treat medical ailments, he has also gifted therapists and counselors to help with emotional support.

How do I find a grief support group?

Your local church or local hospice centers in your area may offer grief groups.

What happens in a grief support group?

You may receive external support during your loss. This group is led by a mental health professional or a volunteer, in some settings. You may be around others who have experienced loss and will receive support from those who have experienced various types of loss.

Author's Note

In writing this memoir, I have recreated details and conversations from my own memory. In order to maintain the anonymity of those involved in my memories, I have, in certain situations, changed the names of individuals or places. I may have also compressed timelines in service of the reading experience. The tips at the back of this memoir are for informational purposes only and do not replace or substitute enlisting with mental health services, if warranted. The list of resources and information is not an endorsement but a collection of resources that I utilized to help me during my journey.

Reflections and Notes

Reflections and Notes

Reflections and Notes

CPSIA information can be obtained
at www.ICGtesting.com
Printed in the USA
BVHW091059080922
646559BV00016B/783